Cool

REFASHIONED
SWEATERS

FUN & EASY FASHION PROJECTS

ALEX KUSKOWSKI

Checkerboard Library

An Imprint of Abdo Publishing
abdopublishing.com

abdopublishing.com

Published by Abdo Publishing, a division of ABDO,
PO Box 398166, Minneapolis, Minnesota 55439.
Copyright © 2016 by Abdo Consulting Group, Inc.
International copyrights reserved in all countries. No
part of this book may be reproduced in any form without
written permission from the publisher. Checkerboard
Library™ is a trademark and logo of Abdo Publishing.

Printed in the United States of America,
North Mankato, Minnesota

062015
092015

THIS BOOK CONTAINS
RECYCLED MATERIALS

Content Developer: Nancy Tuminelly
Design and Production: Jen Schoeller, Mighty Media, Inc.
Series Editor: Liz Salzmann
Photo Credits: Jen Schoeller, Shutterstock

The following manufacturers/names appearing in this
book are trademarks: Rit® Liquid Dye

Library of Congress
Cataloging-in-Publication Data

Kuskowski, Alex, author.
Cool refashioned sweaters : fun & easy fashion
projects / Alex Kuskowski.
      pages cm. -- (Cool refashion)

Audience: Grades 4 to 6.
Includes index.
ISBN 978-1-62403-704-7

1. Sweaters--Juvenile literature. 2. Dress
accessories--Juvenile literature. 3. Fashion design-
-Juvenile literature. 4. Handicraft for girls--Juvenile
literature. I. Title.

TT825.K875 2016
646.4--dc23
                              2014045322

To Adult Helpers

This is your chance to assist a new crafter! As children learn to craft, they develop new skills, gain confidence, and make cool things. These activities are designed to help children learn how to make their own craft projects. They may need more assistance for some activities than others. Be there to offer guidance when they need it. Encourage them to do as much as they can on their own. Be a cheerleader for their creativity.

Before getting started, remember to lay down ground rules for using tools and supplies and for cleaning up. There should always be adult supervision when using a sharp tool.

Table of Contents

RESTART YOUR WARDROBE

Turn Sweaters  Sweet Stuff

Get started refashioning! Refashioning is all about reusing things you already have. You can turn them into new things that you'll love.

Reuse sweaters by remaking them. Use sweaters to make mittens or boots. Or just make it look like a new sweater.

Permission & Safety

- Always get **permission** before making crafts at home.

- Ask whether you can use the tools and materials needed.

- Ask for help if you need it.

- Be careful with sharp and hot objects such as knives and irons.

Be Prepared

- Read the entire activity before you begin.

- Make sure you have everything you need to do the project.

- Follow directions carefully.

- Clean up after you are finished.

Basic terms and step-by-step instructions will make redoing your closet a breeze. These projects will help you turn sweaters into one-of-a-kind fashion pieces.

DON'T SWEAT IT

REmakE iT

Sweaters are a great source of fabric! If you have a sweater that's old, stained, or too small, you can reuse it for the fabric. Make new things with scissors, glue, string, and a little **imagination!**

WORKING WITH SWEATERS

IF POSSIBLE, USE FABRIC SCISSORS. THEY ARE MADE FOR CUTTING FABRIC.

WASH ALL SWEATERS BEFORE YOU USE THEM IN CRAFT PROJECTS.

DRAW WHERE YOU WILL CUT WITH CHALK FIRST TO AVOID MAKING MISTAKES.

Refashion Ideas for Sweaters

WOOL WONDERS

- Wash an old wool sweater in hot water to make felt.
- **Unravel** an old sweater and use the yarn for fun projects.

SUPER SCISSORS

- Cut up an old sweater. Use the scraps to decorate other clothes.
- Cut the sleeves off an old sweater to make a vest.

SEW NEW

- Sew patches on an old sweater.
- Sew sweater fabric into mittens, hats, and **scarves**.

TOOLS & MATERIALS

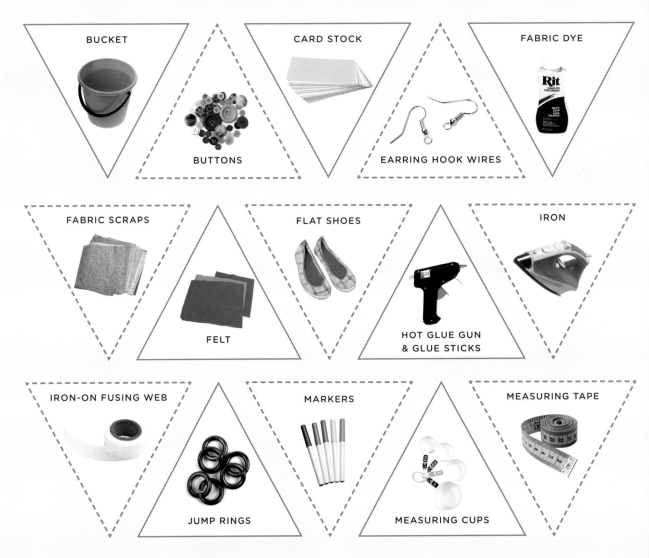

BUCKET

BUTTONS

CARD STOCK

EARRING HOOK WIRES

FABRIC DYE

FABRIC SCRAPS

FELT

FLAT SHOES

HOT GLUE GUN & GLUE STICKS

IRON

IRON-ON FUSING WEB

JUMP RINGS

MARKERS

MEASURING CUPS

MEASURING TAPE

HERE ARE SOME OF THE THINGS YOU'LL NEED FOR THE PROJECTS IN THIS BOOK.

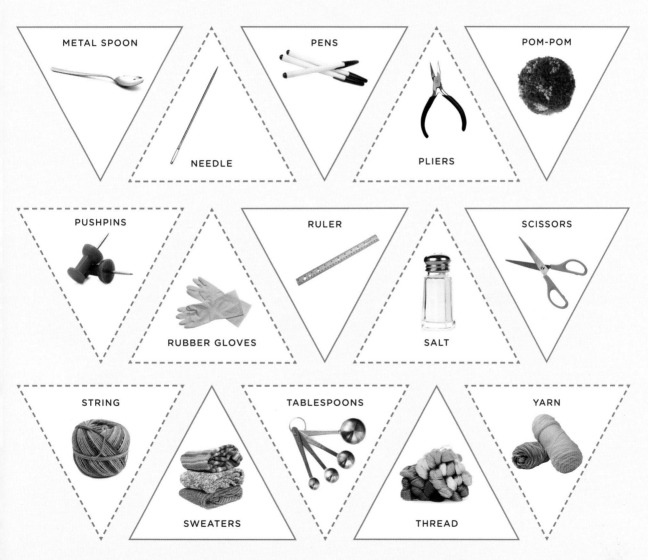

METAL SPOON

NEEDLE

PENS

PLIERS

POM-POM

PUSHPINS

RUBBER GLOVES

RULER

SALT

SCISSORS

STRING

SWEATERS

TABLESPOONS

THREAD

YARN

ALL-TIED-UP SWEATER

Make a Trendy Sweater!

WHAT YOU NEED

FELT
MEASURING TAPE
SCISSORS
IRON-ON FUSING WEB
(ONE SIDE ADHESIVE)
IRON
MARKER
SWEATER
NEEDLE
THREAD

1. Cut a 12-inch (30 cm) square out of felt. Iron one-sided fusing web to one side of the felt. Follow the instructions on the package.

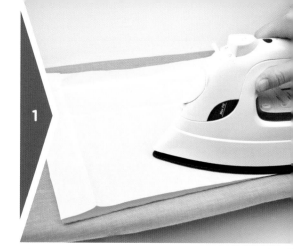

2. Draw a bow on the fusing web. Cut out the bow.

3. Peel the paper off the fusing web. Place the bow on the sweater with the fusing web facing down. Iron it in place.

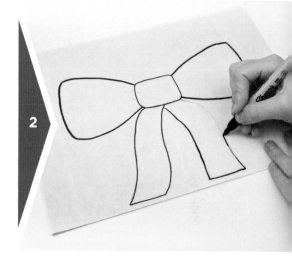

4. Thread the needle. Tie a knot at one end of the thread. Sew around the edges to make it look more finished.

Even Cooler!

Draw different shapes. Try drawing a heart, a star, or letter!

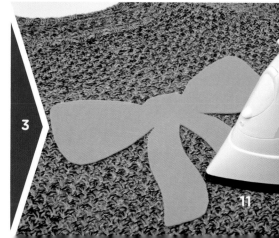

PERFECT
MITTS

Get Smitten with These Mittens!

WHAT YOU NEED

PAPER

MARKER

SCISSORS

SWEATER

NEEDLE

STRING

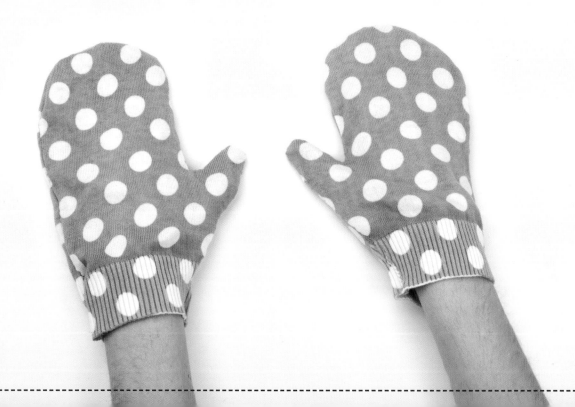

1. Place your hand on a sheet of paper. Trace a mitten shape around your hand. Make sure to leave a little extra space around your hand. Cut out the shape.

2. Place the mitten shape on the sweater. Line the bottom of the mitten up with the hem of the sweater. Cut around the shape through both layers of the sweater. Turn the shape over. Keep it lined up with the sweater's hem. Cut around it again.

3. Match a fabric mitten from each cutting together. Line them up with the front of the fabric facing in.

4. Thread the needle with string. Tie a knot at one end of the string. Sew around the outside of the mitten. Leave the bottom edge open. Turn the mitten right side out.

5. Repeat step 4 with the other two cutouts to sew a matching mitten.

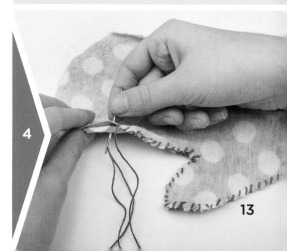

13

COZY HEADBAND

Keep Warm and Look Good!

WHAT YOU NEED

MEASURING TAPE

PAPER

PEN

SWEATER

SCISSORS

NEEDLE

STRING

FABRIC SCRAP

HOT GLUE GUN & GLUE STICKS

1. Measure your head where a headband would go. Add 1 inch (2.5 cm). Write down the total measurement.

2. Cut a rectangle out of the sweater. Make it 8 inches (20 cm) wide and your total measurement long.

3. Fold the rectangle in half **lengthwise**. Make sure the front of the fabric is facing in. Thread the needle with string. Tie a knot at one end of the string. Sew the long edges together.

4. Turn the fabric right side out. Lay it down with the seam in the center. Bring the ends together. Sew all four layers together.

5. Cut one long strip out of the sweater and one out of a fabric scrap. Make them both 1 by 20 inches (2.5 by 51 cm).

6. Tie one end of each long strip together. Twist the two strips together. Wrap the twisted fabric around the knot. Glue it in place as you wrap to make a **rosette**.

7. Glue the rosette to the headband. Let the glue dry.

DaRLiNG
DANGLING EARRINGS

Remake a Sweater into Jewelry!

WHAT YOU NEED

WOOL SWEATER

CARD STOCK

RULER

SCISSORS

PUSHPIN

4 JUMP RINGS

PLIERS

2 EARRING HOOK WIRES

1. Wash the sweater in a washing machine with hot water and high **agitation**. Let it dry.

2. Cut a teardrop shape out of card stock. Make it at least 2 inches (5 cm) long. Place the shape on the sweater. Cut the sweater around the shape. Cut a second teardrop out of the sweater the same way.

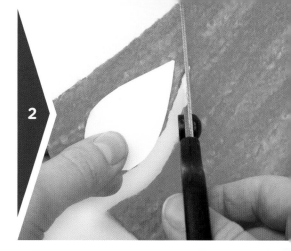

3. Use the pushpin to poke a hole through the point of a fabric teardrop.

4. Open a jump ring with the pliers. Put the ring through the hole in the teardrop. Close the ring. Open another jump ring. Put it through the first ring and the earring hook wire. Close the ring.

5. Repeat steps 3 and 4 to make a matching earring.

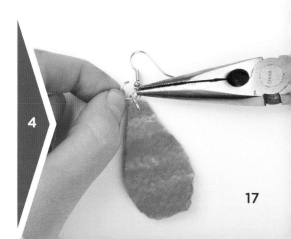

SNOWY DAY HAT

Make a Cute Cozy Cap!

WHAT YOU NEED

SWEATER
RULER
SCISSORS
NEEDLE
THREAD
POM-POM

1. Lay the sweater out flat. Cut two half-circles out of the bottom of the sweater. Make them 9 inches (23 cm) wide and 7 inches (18 cm) high.

2. Cut a triangle out of the top of each half-circle. The triangle should be 3 by 3 inches (8 by 8 cm).

3. Fold a half-circle in half with the front of the fabric facing in. Thread the needle. Tie a knot at one end of the thread. Sew along the edges of the triangle. Repeat with the other half-circle.

4. Unfold the half-circles. Lay them on top of each other with the fronts facing each other. Sew around the sides and top.

5. Turn the hat right side out. Sew the pom-pom to the top of the hat.

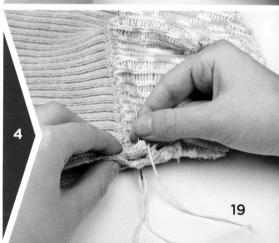

19

SNUGGLE-UP Socks

You'll Love Showing Off Your New Socks!

WHAT YOU NEED

SWEATER

SCISSORS

RULER

MARKER

NEEDLE

YARN

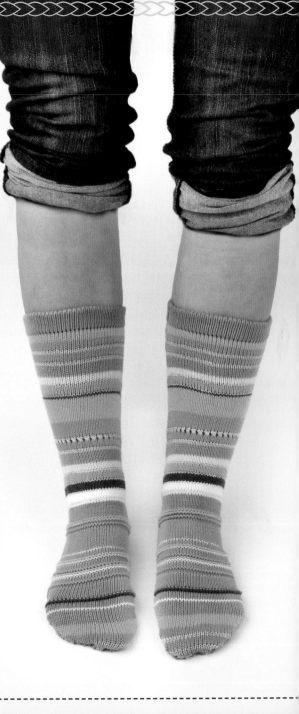

1. Cut the sleeves off the sweater.

2. Turn the sleeves inside out. Put your feet through the cuffs. Pull the sleeves up your legs. Stop when about 1 inch (2.5 cm) of fabric hangs over your toes. Make sure the seams are on the outside edges of your feet.

3. Draw around the front of each foot with a marker. Take off the sleeves.

4. Cut along the lines. Make sure you cut through both layers of fabric.

5. Thread the needle with yarn. Tie a knot at one end of the yarn. Sew the curved edges together. Turn the socks right side out.

21

COWL
SCARF WRAP

Get Warm with a Cool Wrap!

WHAT YOU NEED

WOOL SWEATER

SCISSORS

RULER

IRON-ON FUSING WEB

IRON

FABRIC SCRAPS

BUTTON

NEEDLE

STRING

1. Wash the sweater in a washing machine with hot water and high **agitation**. Let it dry.

2. Cut the bottom of the sweater off under the arms.

3. Turn the bottom of the sweater inside out. Put fusing web 1 inch (2.5 cm) from the cut edge. Fold the edge of the sweater over the fusing web. Iron it in place following the instructions on the package.

4. Cut three circles out of fabric scraps. Make them different sizes.

5. **Stack** the circles from largest to smallest. Place the button on top. Sew the button on through all of the layers of fabric.

6. Thread the needle with string. Tie a knot at one end of the string. Pinch a little bit of the **cowl** together in the middle. Sew the stack of circles onto the pinched fabric.

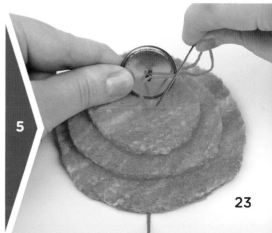

23

COLOR-CHANGING
SWEATER

Get Your Fashion On!

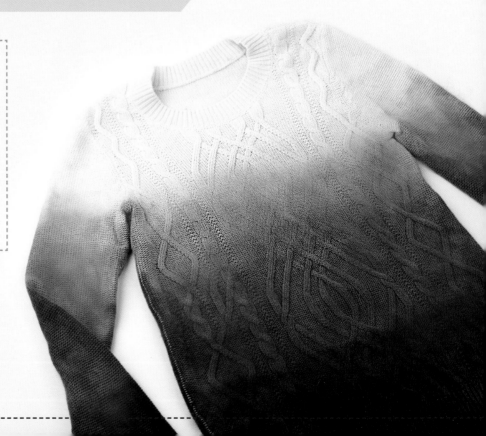

WHAT YOU NEED

LIGHT-COLORED SWEATER

RUBBER GLOVES

BUCKET

MEASURING CUP

RIT DYE

TABLESPOON

SALT

LARGE METAL SPOON

1 Wash the sweater in warm water. Leave it wet.

2 Put on rubber gloves. Put ½ cup dye, 6 tablespoons salt, and 6 cups hot water in the bucket. Stir with a metal spoon.

3 Put the bottom fourth of the sweater in the dye. **Soak** it for 15 minutes.

4 Put the bottom half of the sweater in the dye for 10 minutes. Put three-fourths of the sweater into the dye for 4 minutes.

5 Remove the sweater from the dye. Wring out any extra dye. Rinse the sweater under cold water. Hold it by the shoulders so the dye runs down toward the bottom. Rinse it until the water becomes clear. Let the sweater dry.

6 Machine wash it alone to rinse out the remaining dye.

Cute
SWEATER
BOOTS

Kick It up a Notch!

1 Cut the sleeves off the sweater along the seams.

2 Line the seam of a sleeve up with the heel of a shoe. Hot glue the seam to the center of the heel.

3 Wrap the cut edge of the sleeve around the shoe.

CONTINUED ON NEXT PAGE

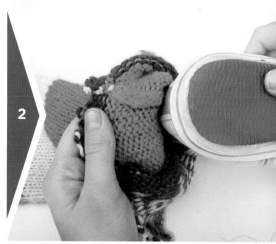

4 Roll the cut edge of the sleeve under ½ inch (1 cm). Line it up with the bottom edge of the shoe.

5 Glue 1 inch (2.5 cm) of the edge of the sleeve to the shoe.

6 Glue the sleeve the rest of the way around the shoe. Glue it 1 inch (2.5 cm) at a time.

7 Fold the cuff of the sleeve down 4 inches (10 cm). Stretch the cuff with your hands.

8 Thread the needle with string. Tie a knot at one end of the string. Sew the edge of the cuff to the sleeve. Knot the string. Cut off the extra string.

9 Sew two buttons to the cuff on the outside of the boot.

10 Repeat steps 2 through 9 to make the other boot.

CoNCLUSioN

Congratulations! You've just completed some fun projects using sweaters. But don't stop here! Take what you've learned to the next step. Try out your own ideas for refashioning sweaters. Make something **unique** and totally you!

Check out the other books in this series. Learn how to refashion jeans, **scarves**, T-shirts, and more.

Get crafting today!

GLOSSARY

AGITATION – the act of moving or stirring something with a jerky motion.

COWL – a high, loose collar.

IMAGINATION – the creative ability to think up new ideas and form mental images of things that aren't real or present.

LENGTHWISE – in the direction of the longest side.

PERMISSION – when a person in charge says it's okay to do something.

ROSETTE – an ornament fabric or ribbon gathered or wound into a circle.

SCARF – a long piece of cloth worn around the neck for decoration or to keep warm.

SOAK – to leave something in a liquid for a while.

STACK – 1. to put things in a pile. 2. a pile of things placed one on top of the other.

UNIQUE – different, unusual, or special.

UNRAVEL – to come apart or to come undone.

Websites

To learn more about Cool Refashion, visit **booklinks.abdopublishing.com**. These links are routinely monitored and updated to provide the most current information available.

iNDeX